For Zuri Yvette,

My Favourite Poet

Poems by Jodie Moss

Transcribed, edited and foreword by Jorge Moss

Additional transcription by Alix Harrington

Dear Reader.

Jodie left a lot of poems after her death in March of 2016. 3 notebooks brimming with her work; her schedules, her notes, her life and her mind. These poems are one of the best insights into who Jodie really was, as a daughter, as a partner and as my sister. Most importantly though, as a person. Her own person.

Soon after finding all the works myself and my family began saying we wanted to get them published, believing them too important, not just to us but in general, for their merit, to leave unknown and un-proliferated.

We loved Jodie dearly, however it becomes very apparent very quickly in her work that she was not well, that she struggled greatly with her own mind. Not to romanticize the issue, but this made Jodie not dissimilar to many of her idols, even from poetry. Jodie looked up to the likes of Oscar Wilde and Sylvia Plath, who famously took her own life.

Jodie was without a doubt the best big sister I could have ever asked for. I used to call her Little Mummy when we were young. And she, ever the fiercely intelligent and independent soul, informed my mother she did not know how to look after me. Jodie was no older than 5 at the time and I was only a tiny baby.

Jodie will be forever missed. I, her Mum, her Dad, Callum, Wilbur, her Grandparents, Willow and countless others will mark every day she is gone. I will always maintain it was the hardest thing I have ever has to do, to carry my sisters coffin and read her eulogy, but to read some of the poems in this compilation has been harrowing to say the least.

Many hours of work have gone into typing up these poems with nothing to say of the tears. I hope however, you think no differently of Jodie upon reading these however, as she is still the same Jodie you knew. You'll just know more about her. And with knowledge I hope will come respect and a new love and admiration for the incredibly strong person she was.

It must be noted however that apart from some adjustments to spelling, the layout and wording of each poem remains exactly as found. To remain true to both the vision and the mind that wrote them. This may make for some odd structuring.

Everyone who needs to know knows what happened to Jodie in the end and throughout her life, so I will not cover that. Instead, this is a celebration of her written art, which may lead one to ponder the name given to the compilation.

The name is one of Jodie's choosing. It was written on the first page of one notebook. It was on the first page of the collection of poems she had printed. I do not know where the name came from however, I do recall her saying it was her. In a sense.

Lastly, thank you so much to one of my best friends Alix, without whom it would have taken far longer and been far more draining to fulfil this take.

I also took the liberty of composing two of my own poems at the end. One for how her loss is felt, and one for the simple act that took it.

Love you Jodie

Jorge, her little brother (bother)

CONTENTS

FOR ZURI YVETTE, MY FAVOURITE POET

This was to be a poem,
to tell you how I feel.
This was to be a hymn,
to something strange but red.
But I've not the words,
too many voices in my mind.
I'm broken-down, always afraid,
But you've always been kind,
Accepting, loving, full of grace,
Poised and Pretty, fair of face.
I miss you now, far more than most.
And dread the day I kiss your Ghost.

MON NOUVEAU COPAINS

Because sometimes poetry deserves a pretentious French
title.

If I can liquidize aggression,
Laugh it off at late:
A want to be in concession,
To play, to participate.
Such is the irritants,
Squirming involuntary,
Doubt of reminiscence,
Anything to not be solitary.
Confide in being extroverted,
Confess a dirty little secret,
Their concepts seem perverted,
There's nothing left but regret.

DIRTY GEESE

I see plenty of rules,
for plenty adaptation of fools,
Here in the Park of Queens.
Where the issues and leaf's fall on deaf ears,
Clutching a four pack of strong own brand beer.

Here in the Park of Queens.
You'd be a king of a queen in this place,
It's a screen and a shelter for the lost human race.
They could move on one day but perhaps they'd rather not.
It's the palace for the people who've accepted their lot.

Here in the Park of Queens.
We'll be here for eons, from 9-10,
Another harsh light and the clock rounds again.
The pain has somewhat subsided to something more crass,
But when morn comes a'slapping we'll still be here on our
ass.

You'd be a king of a queen in this place,
It's a screen and a shelter for the lost human race,
They could move on one day but perhaps they'd rather not.
It's the palace for people who've accepted their lot.

Here in the Park of Queens.
We can't rely on our Gender to get through.
There's monarchy harlots with faces un-new,

Are worn down as their stilettos and toys-
The faces of men withered with the shallow hearts of boys.

You'd be a king of a queen in this place,
It's a screen and a shelter for the lost human race.
They could move on one day but perhaps they'd rather not.
It's the palace for the people who've accepted their lot.
Here in the Park of Queens.

THEM

Triple distilled
In the eyes of Men,
Polluted distastefully
In the eyes of Men.
Reminisce of a time Men didn't exist.
Fun didn't exist.
Fun isn't fun without responsibility to
Ignore.
Ignorance is triple distilled
In the eyes of Men.
Ignorance of Men.
Oh God,
Men.
Triple polluted
By the eyes of Men.
The distasteful fun of ignorant Men.
Tasteful fun does not exist.
Tasteful men do not exist.
What's responsible for the polluted hearts of
Men
In the eyes of Men?

I WON'T APOLOGISE FOR PATTERNS

I'll enjoy my own voice,
As it comes through in verse.
Heed my own advice that things could be worse.
And although my rhyme
Seems to follow the same beat,
This is okay, It's the rhythm of my feet.

OWNER'S RESULT

A pictorial memorial
For a life
Still in play.
A walk,
A drink,
another crumpled day.
Stream the lines.
The track will run a backwards car.

The mimesis of the moth;
We're living just because we are.

Says I taste of sweetened anti-septic.

Flushed flesh.
Chiastic pose.
Noir delight.
We are cantered.

Reward can be a sickened play thing.
Grubby girl.
Told her ribboning plaits would wither
If she dare be impure.

BATH

From the tear duck of the tap
To my personal sea.
How's an hour considering drowning to dispel one's
misery?
'Hey you there!' beckons the bottom of the tub.
I'll pretend I didn't hear.
Through guilt to wish to follow rather than from fear.
I crave a sleep,
Two foot manipulated by three.
I'll bathe again tomorrow, it can't kill me.

MORNING ROUTINE

Fluted barely human figure,
My being in a bounce of soleil.
A screwed up ordinate survey map
Smoothed out in vein
By hands as marred.
Bristled weapon tames reality,
Likewise, a varnish conceals the façade.
Once made from liquid infant rabbits.
Blame their obituaries for possibility to
Escape.

PERSPIRING PIKE

We're pilgrims from here,
Wherever we are,
To get nowhere.
But the perception is it's everywhere.
Occult, ill-lit but could well have been
The most luminous mid-summers day.
We fell like autumnal foliage
From cliff to burning core.
Sinking most pleasurably.
Contact most unmeaningful,
Though we could be paranoid.
Skin on skin
But deeper still.
The company dreadfully perfect.
The morning hours sprint away
With burdened breath.
To terminate would be a great tragedy.
Recurrence uncertain,
Perhaps we like it this way.

CATACLYSMIC MASQUERADES

I too am on a ship belayed and calmed.
An Iago or sorts in a tragedy all of my own.
I abhor those who tell me this is not the way things are.
My own self-pity is all the concern I can withstand.
I've a preferment of those who feel quite the same.
And I'll always say 'God bless those who resign to atheism.
A trust in religion is as absurd as a trust in politics.
I am not what I am,
Through no fault of another,
Hence my honesty be viewed as a more worthy of masks.

RHETORIC TOWN

It's cascading mundane.
Fenestration opaque.
70's but with no sign of flare.
Crazy pave your psyche
Add dot it with gum
This is the place we call
Home.
A replica of all others
But the stooges differ in name.
Just about.
Synchronized steps on a marathon to order.
Individuality purged on rollies
And cheap Vodka.
You would think the queue for the Why
Would detach the parasites.

SHE'LL FEEL BETTER

I tore a line from my own song.
I sang it loud all evening long.
He heard my voice,
He mocked my skill,
He swore the line was perfect still.
I scratched this line on all my skin,
Reassurance of my beauty, proof;
But when he did remove my clothes,
He said my line was not the truth.

LACHRYMAL SECRETION

Pendant glass are you chained to my sockets?
So very permanent.
Kinetics tear the tissue.
I use so very much of
That.
Hold it back, hold it back, hold it back.
HOLD
IT
BACK!
You're so weak.
Well are you not?
Imprison the Bulbus Oculi.
Ally a substance other than my own.
Others see the picture dans peinture claire-
Why not you my darling flower?

AINT WORKING

Chop and change a rhythm,
Build to a structure again.
Swap and alter the pattern,
Like the hearts and minds of
Men.
Count the syllables thrice,
To note down 8 and 9,
Re-read as an obsession,
Now ensure it's all in time.
Don't Flipping Bother.
If it's right it's right.
No one who reads it cares,
Only you... But then again they might...

HERE IN MY PART OF THE WORLD

Florescent colour,
A vivid rouge and indigo-
Miraculous really.
Slabs an unforgiving chess board.
I am the pawn.
Let the monarchy leave
Bruises of earthly tones.
It's all in the aggregate
Of these bound and stitched up
Phobias.
Not a tipple nor a better kind of emerald,
The only thing felt;
A head rush in our pocket.
Retched sky you dilate pupils.
Very much surviving but hardly living.

BITCH

The mind of a Bitch in the body of a Bitch,
With the heart of a pressed daisy petal,
Dry freezed.
If it were possible for me to run circles around your soul.
To trample you down,
I'd be pleased.
Only if this didn't wreck myself,
I've a conscience you know
I can never quite get around.
I aim to be cold, uncaring aloof;
But foremost I sense my chest pound.
It's not due to you as a specific you see,
The man is the varying factor.
I've been built all wrong.
My wires are crossed.
I shall focus on my Bitch on the contractor.

GETTING THERE

We'll guild it with shit
And betray our roots as the great Oscar did,
But in reverse.
We'll strive to be poor,
To be walked over,
Walked over,
Struggle,
Barely get by
But have fun
No time is free time.
We must get on this crap every day.
We'll pretend we aspire-
And maybe we once did.
But we aint got common through long term dreams.

PERCEPTION FLAWED?

They have a word for them,
Like you.
A label forced on and sticky.
No amount of spirit can remove this glue-
Good reputations may prove tricky.
So raise a hand if alone
And muster the courage to not obey.
Don't think of your idiolect,
Your dress,
You're friends,
And the image you might portray.
"Your hair and shoes are just so wrong,
Your life must surely follow too.
Guard your real self,
From fear of the Jury,
Whatever, just don't be you."

FAITH

Someone once told me
to believe in
God
"It's fun, try it-
See if God <u>wants you</u>
To believe
In Him."
So I did. It was fun.
But
He didn't.

FATHER LUNE

Your greying hair is no wisdom.
Your hollowed space dust face denotes
No hard life,
Only hard heart
You charm,
Allow mellower clouds to pass you
You deny them no
Their superficial win is your cover;
It hides your scowl.

But when you so wish,
You can block the prettiest Sun.
You eclipse her
An angered umbra
Stop the world receiving her-
It is your desire.

You are no light source.
You emit not your own energy
Only the luminosity you assimilate
Drain,
Squander,
From that you surround yourself with.
You project their happiness back at them,
Mocking their now lost spirit.

You do cause this romantic adumbration
Both the affection and chalky vague
Instruction.

You are the symbol of dark.
The ugly,
The sad,
The lonely,
The show themselves to them,
In dim, kinder light
But reveal them none the less.

Where you are pure Beauty
From the Eve of time
Where all take for granted you will be there
To whistle defiled lullabies at night.
I fear the chance you will not appear,
Be incapacitated,
Or simply choose not.
We need not constant, honest Sun
And all must sleep
However unsettled.

MISS MUFFET

Sat with spiders the cigarettes down beside her
She pulled from her throat
a note.
It read,

I'm part of the nursery,
My thoughts all in
rhyme
I've crossed the lips of children
and mothers through time.
Just as a fable, read then
put on the table
the fear of the most, an effortless
ghost, who will not touch hearts many words apart
only a story, I'm written not
real, people oblivious to that
I may too feel
a need for a song to get
me to sleep,
just as does boo peep alone with her
sheep.
This is the day I denounce
my place.
I take up a knife and slip
far from grace,
Isn't it weird how only she whose dead?
has a face.
I'm bled childhood dreams
all over my tuffet
So long cruel world.

Much love,
                Miss Muffet.

UNTITLED 2

We ridicule the Sun
Sea and Earth
The women who gives us birth
The educators who bore
The ones who impassion music, film, fashion,
And slate poor and wealthy
the sick and healthy
The mentally stable, the quite insane
the ones who care and the ones
who cause pain.
We mock all the professions done well
or not
Humanity coats objects, places and people
with rot
Declaring they're awful, boring, shit
But not all people care to admit
That they, them, I, you
Are the epitome of mistakes
But realising this flaw is just
what it takes
To make the world just a little
darker and sad
These seers see all, and they're
confirmed it's all bad.

I remember a day
I do!
a memory so pure
it hurts to think of
it again
So dirty you wish
It never happened.
So sordid
You wish it was canned
But beautiful
We drank
 As you don't do anymore
We talked
Not fought
And things were perfect `

UNTITLED 3 (VERSION 2)

I remember a day
I do!
A memory so pure
It hurts to think of
It again
So dirty you wish
It never happened
So scared/sordid
You wish it was
But beautiful
We drank

EVERYTHING IS POETRY

He told me
"Stop living a poetical dream"
I said I and romance in all
poetry is romance.
There is romance in everything.
Every hurt, Every line
Every mundane thought
Taking a shower
A quick one-off hat
Squishing a spider under a
heavy heeled boot
EVERYTHING IS POETRY

LETTERS

I'm always writing letters
I never mean to send
To knights in white satin,
With kisses at the end.
P.S I promise
Our nylon nights aren't
through
I've stamped the wax to seal
the lie
To know it will come true.
I'm always writing letters
and some of them have sent
to the one valiant and genuine
creature
to whom these words aren't meant.

UNTITLED 5

As jails are built from layers of brick,
people are built from layers of mistakes.
The more mistakes you learn from,
the higher you become,
the greater you grow as a person.
Oh, we learn and many mistakes We'll never repeat,
but we seem to find worse to commit,
not physically but mentally.
I find myself crumbling,
getting shorter by the day, like many.
These prisons walls are
falling and the criminals
are loose and
thirsty for blood, spunk.

UNTITLED 6

Slumped in the corner
is the only man who
says he loves you.
The flickering candles
through lanterns
cast shadows on his
face more playful
than his expression.
The furrow of his brow
is anger at your upset.
His anger upsets.
There's too much upset
For a man who says
He loves you.

UNTITLED 7

You're my Sweetest Mistake,
A Risk Proud to Take. Fill Me
At thy leisure. My Purest
Pleasure, My ice-cream heart Ache.
When my ace
Digits fat with numbness
I'm so little but swollen.

JORGE

Look up my boy!
Look up to the light.
Those orbiting citadels will inspire flight.
The stars look far
But for you they're more near
For you, my brother,
Are lacking that fear,
That scally's over compensate
For and makes morality near.
We can aspire to be anything
But not all will succeed;
For you there is only hope,
For you will lead
With a smile as wide
As the sky, itself
You will fall into greatness,
Love and wealth.
You're young my boy
Just a broad-shouldered sprout
But all see your grandeur,
And there is no doubt,
You'll be something special,
You can have all you desire.
Just continue with your optimism
And your heart full of fire.

RENAISSANCE LOVE

It came from flighty touches
We came with not so flighty gestures
New and known simultaneously.
Aware without past.
Memories for the unborn.
We may have made too many.
It only takes a step
But a large and spontaneous lunge
In shores to match the ego
Of a couple dons armour.
Armour of strongest bronze
May we never be poor;
Lacking of Love
Lacking of heart
Never alone, never to part.

UNTITLED 8

This violent bond
of messy agendas.
Oiled and waxed to
groomed, dirty splendours.
Time is our friend
our enemy is yester year
Our promise is our parting fear
This affection is
to the eyes what it is to
my skin
Bluer than blue
But thicker than sin.
I am yet to heal
Yet to heel
Heel to me
Our pact is sworn!

UNTITLED 9

I heel to grit.
Always burnt and forgiven
Not forgotten,
Drunk Darwin.
See me now as I see you.
Rosy pink forever true.

Caress the mess
that is my mind
You'll touch a nerve
to serve and find
a secret source
to all I adore
a perfect mistake
in all that's a flaw
We are all the same
ruined but gained, you and i
through knowledge and pain
let me transplant
my heart in your hearts place
So you can feel what
leaves distain on my face

UNTITLED 11

The constant insistence
on perfection
exhausts one's optimism.
The eyes turn dull
the smile sags
the brain a cataclysm.
Oh, how standards
warp the world.
The good is not up to expectations
and how this life, these
looks and job
sacrifice relations.
A want of higher life is
imminent and so your dreams,
they cry. Your perceptions of
your deserving are wrong, a hedonistic lie.

UNTITLED 12

I kneel before my Lord
I pray on all fours
Or on my back
Always praying, though
The serpent tempts me to
that trimmed Eden
And on forbidden fruit
I sup'
Give me this day my daily bread
As you deliver me to evil
Not my father, my son but
Holy Ghost, Holy Lover
"Oh God." List for me all
commandments.

UNTITLED 13

My faith is strong
My body hot, yet you'll
Perform for me one miracle Not?
Amen.
A man.
My man.

UNTITLED 14

The couples Trinity is complete
By the girl
The boy and
The Holy Lay.

THE WEST FOLLOW...

They all fain of West
In the battle of the
      connoisseurs
None knowing even
      texture from taste
They lack specific pallet
      talent
But have ability to
      spend at haste.

UNTITLED 15

Calibrated differences
equal harmony
But a fear of future
Conflict causes present
tension.
My Irritability

UNTITLED 16

My smile is expensive
It costs more than
love.

When a shoulder drops
She falls, twice as hard
Twice as far,
But it's not the hands
That fire,
That char.
like an ambulance
Acceptor of lame
Injured not to help
neglectful by name.
I scold the patient
if she does not hurt herself
enough
provide the instruments
That make their lives so tough
I peeked through the fence
Wednesdayism, gown clad, belly down
to witness the pretence
of the cured,
the healed clowns
in the Garden where
man first found pleasure.
Was knocked back by a
peculiar measure
of tranquilised instruction
and the hand of my own sire
The very same one she saw
die just prior. It just goes to
show that your efforts are a
waste.

UNTITLED 18

He will not remember Her
But never forget the way
Her tears taste.

UNTITLED 19

You are a concept
you know so
You've done the lot
the crack the blow
and now you must
give up your life
like
drink, a thing you "should
miss" in time.
I am criminal
I am against the law
despite the program
and will
I've hit a load
I'm addicted I hurt
To heal I fail. My life
Is worth nothing at all.

MY SOLDIER AND I

We've seen stars and sunrise,
Dusk through to daw
Endured substance to save
Us from yawn.
We've seen wax splattered peaks
That run into rivers,
Where the water snake hides,
Wriggles and slithers,
And coughs up salt water
Into the throat of the girl
Who saves the taste
And transforms it into a pearl
That she heaps into her oyster
That sings of that name
Without it hopeless and with it in shame
Distress is the best form of refrain.
Leaving and crying, avoiding such pain
Neither one believes the other,
Though all truth is told,
The Adoration does not,
But the Topics get old.

Can you fathom the
glitters I've seen?
Now I'm without sparkle?
the depth in-between,
 that section where the
corner of light is canto.
The edge of the sequin
the gathered greed primal
to say down to go down
try it once deer,
just do!
With a crusted clown,
Painted tears,
Leaving on you.

UNTITLED 21

Smack it out of her
Watch the confidence loss
She'll adore you more
If you show her whose boss.
She'll assume it's a joke
It's a pleasurable act
But you'll know what you mean
by this condemning pact.

THE REAL ME:

I've no persona to call my own,
I've stolen a trait a view or a tone.
I'm the Frankenstein's monster of ways to be perceived.
I'm so muddled up I've even got myself deceived.
I'll love you one month and maybe even like me,
But the next I've moved on to a new fabricated reality.
It's all real at the time but I've never had my own mind-
I'm a self-manufactured machine on the rapid unwind.

UNTITLED 22

I loved everything about you
that hurt
I've seen your moves, you've seen
I was told I was Alice
In a wonderland I couldn't dare
exit

From pillar to post
Dirty and stained
Chilly but numbed
The vin shared
and dousing last nights
poison.
The tracks so cold
On naked back.
We wouldn't die
Would we?

UNTITLED 24

I scorned at him, I've done this
before but never actually waited
for the train to get so close.
His hand was in mine. As I
Found the image of a couple
led on the rail tracks connected
by an outstretched arm, irresistibly
Romantic. Playing with their lives
But caring little, desperately Romantic
A head light of the vehicle
peered round the corner of a bush.
We count from ten... by the time the
5 second maker hits I've got an
energy serge. The train is closer than
it should be but I'm glued to
the track. We will not move.
Ten. We stand, best scuffle over
gravel to the edge where the
grass meets the line. My hair
is dragged left by
pull of the speeding train.
I looked at him, that man, and
saw a grin spread across his
stubbled face. "The driver did this at
us!" he says, making the "wanker"
hand signal. I laugh and shrink
"well we are a bit."
But I was happy.
I was happy when I woke up
Near to him that morning, Happy
making him bacon sandwiches.

Ecstatic when he stole my underwear
To wear for the day. I wasn't to
Know this was just the beginning
of the days magic.

I just can't write when
My thoughts are abundant
With empty.
The fact I'm putting this
On paper contradicts this.
This is me when I'm not
Entirely present.
When creativity is dry.
So why do I still write?
Still?
Because I can, my
thoughts were set free
and so I want to keep my hand.
Like an 80's soap opera
Mixed with a drug movie.
Faint smell of cannabis
and the crest in odd socks
They've mismatching sofas
that fit so well together.
A gun fire sounds but it's
On the TV.
Eyes red and staring at
nothing. A concentration
on something withdrawn.
These are the people of
the world but not the worlds people.

There is no light at
the end of the tunnel,
Only a bright beautiful
Mess
But the sooner I follow
the light the sooner I'll
be a little bit beautiful.
Long live
the car crash
fleets.

UNTITLED 27

je suis une
magnifique socle
et je voudrais
etre une luna
mais je ne
pense pas
que que je voudrais
faire

I am a
beautiful base
and I would like
to be a moon
but I do not think
that I would
like to do

UNTITLED 28

I'm running out of will
A will for what is real
Only a select few see
the world how it is
it's their curse.
Even fewer of those are
Beautiful.
They're both cursed and
foolish.
But these are the people I
want.
Their company is damning.
But I can damn them
further.
I'm a parasitic cursed fool.

pendant glass chained to
my sockets
so very permanent.
Kinetics tear the tissue
Oh I use so much of
that.
Hold it back
Hold it back
Hold it back
Hold
It
Back
You're so weak.
Imprison the Bulbus Oculi
Alli with a substance
Other than your own
Others see the world class plants dare
Why can't you my darling flower?

UNTITLED 30

Confide in your being extrovert
Confess a dirty secret
If they back away
Hold onto that
Regret

UNTITLED 31

He flounced around
In front of me
I clocked him in an instant
He would not know the
pain I felt
The stabbing as he coned in to
the distance.
I stood in public
And cried for a minute
Followed by a need for drink
I'll miss him
I know I will but the
hurt is more from injustice, I think.

(Three years later; he loves me
I live in Dorset with him and I
cheat. I ruin it all, I'm sick AGAIN.)

UNTITLED 32

Pigeons pigeons
Flap fast
You can't escape
The world dislike has come at last
There're paths to follow
Field to Rome. But if there was ever one
Soon they'll be no home.

"Sentiment is overstated"
He said
£6 for a white gold memory.
2 whiskeys there about
Of a bottle of vodka.
I'll make new memories
not of old.
Sell my soul and history
For a new better day.
A day of joy
dizzy joy.
But we know I'd sell
the world for this day
and con fate
for the next.
Few mean much to me.
But when you do you'll
Know it.
You aim to give me that
dizzy joy for free.
-If I know only one right now who can
This sentience be
greatly underrated, always.
Belittled by those who don't know.
You'll never really know.

UNTITLED 34

Liquid dances on a glass
surface.
Debris shadowing the clarity
perhaps the dirt.
Of 100 poor men
has clouded the view
of the rest.

I LOVE YOU CALLUM

I could have been anything
Maybe even happy.
But I chose to be yours.
You'll be my demise.
But not the death of me.
You help me so much in
the problems you cause.

7:40 was the time.
47 was the win.
3:1 todays similarity.
7 your dropped within
Number 8 a travel still
And 629 is my loved one.
Less year again and he says he
will be game.

WHEN WILL WE REMEMBER?

Calligraphic 'W' on the entrance
Cleaning to serve welcomes
But to me you're only weakness.
A repeat for when the day hell comes
The entrance is also an Exit.
Or an opening to the real fairness

UNTITLED 36

Complimentary corset
And a smile to compliment too
Stand fixated on a message
Board the list a black and monocratic menu

Choose your own fate or
It might become a dissociate.
Focus of a clock and
Find your actions inappropriate

You've been up all night
But that means you were up damned early
You deserve a sit down for your motivation surely.

If another speckled wood
grained saint is going to
remind than everything
you've surrendered should not
result in the unkind

Plasticised leather like a seal
On the root
Remember all things memorable
The exceptions you can 'boot'

UNTITLED 37

It's time to surrender
It's time to review
all the problems you
remember
all the good sins
all the
blue

Swallow pride
and swallow pills
It's a happy song I do swear
and I'll tell you're my
life my darling.

Can I say it? Do I dare?

25 seconds later
and dispute who's in the air
and sort of wonder
I wonder if you
really care.

Oh I've seen a song.
a song about love.
Love song disaster of
an emotion from emote.
Stroll beside me my loved one
and hold me if you will
your actions are so loving
your words so bitter still.

Sometimes we see a puzzle as
Something for fun
But other times it's unworthy
the things that we've undone

UNTITLED 38

We're floating on a
drug riddle raft.
The result unlike an
unwilling suicide is daft

So
 miserable
        and
Stunning.

BOX OFFICE BEAUTIES

We're the touched
We can dress it
with a glossy overcoat
But we'd still be
as rough as splintered
balsa wood.

We're the best at
self-demolition
accessories wrecking
balls on chains.

Dirty
Really
Just dirt.

Pondering the street
as entertainment
for the clean.
They made movies
about us
we watch them sometimes
denying they're
about us
sometimes quote love with
our wrecked selves
But always assured
There's and end
of some sort.

UNTITLED 40

You've another 7 pounds
If you know it.
Of course, you know it
You know within a fraction
Within a salty fraction

UNTITLED 41

Spin it like a
Pizza base
& pray

The ordinary situation
With ordinary lives in two
Cooking, searching
Some want
desperate never with desire to know
some oblige for their weekly
wage.
A call every few days
A beer in all.
A life in none.
And sometimes a fall.
Injustice is what I call it
for I fall every day.
And I work on the constant
Some for which there is no pay
I swore not to eat
Today or a week
But now like a guilt
For this untimely deal
Not even from fridge of
My arm
but causes a welt
of the highest scale
supplying the GDA of a whole
I'll put on some
I need no loose six
Unhappy and fat
It's you who picks
Lonely and unhap

UNTITLED 43

Rancid air
I cannot breathe you
and I do not wish to do so
My open open mouth inhales
But a vacuum
My sound barren vibrations inhibit this
space
No pleading or whispering
draws anyone to help.
Their aid is useless in this underland
Nonetheless the bottle will
make me all and small,
time in all.
I'll vanish to a singular point
In time.
eventually,
inevitably.
They'll miss this blazing
feigned arrogance
their only souvenir a smashed
plate
or an immature condemnation
from barbed tongue.
I'll be a lily
dipped deep in diluted clay.
Fined in passion of 600 degrees,
My odour first cloaked
in early red
burnt and banished to washed
 out beige.
Dusty husk

True life cremated within a

mask.
The outer shell is all that
remains.
 Ready for the rancid air
to blow again
And it will collapse
it-
me.
to unforgiving ash.
Velvet smooth
Through your toes
They'll not cease
To topple. It still feels so good.
For them. Still.

THANK YOU

Gaping toothless mouth
Dry as bix
Coral lips.
Whispered hair strung halfway
back
Complexion as monochrome
Ironically shrouded in pink.
Inhale and exhale
Louder than voice.
Marbled arm
Crooked not by choice
As old as conversation
Still more alike than I.
Scribble circles from tip to elbow
Done for something other than to cry
A symbol for cycles
Cycling fits
Lithium rats.
Three numbers
Talking to her, me, us.
An insomniac causing a fuss
Tasteless coffee
Although black.
I can't digest your
Words
They're too cruel.
 Slag? Plastic? Water?
I wish I was, I'd be
Less dead.
You killed me.
Thank you. They were

Gratefully read.

UNTITLED 45

It's time for the
bright.
That
That was lonely.
I do feel guilty
for the occasion
guilty to enjoy
myself.
But I deserve it.
I understand this
makes for the most
boring poem ever.

SHE WAS SUCH A LOVELY LITTLE GIRL

Red light, fake fur coat
Adorned rights, ten-pound note
Scuffed stilettos, dirty hair.
What the hell's she doing
there?

The
Red fairy lights were the Christmas tree.
Ten-pound gift from Aunty Bessy
Shines and coat stolen from Mummy
The rips in her hair from a fall found funny
What a magic Christmas for
A six-year-old
The outside white with snow.
In ten Christmases time she'll be
Outside, working for her blow.

POSITIONS

Your back,
forever turned to me.
You turn it, so I love you
from a distance.
You turn it when you feel
the space between us
needs lengthening.
You turn mine to
'love' me from behind.
I turn mine so as not to
cry
so you don't see that
pained face. God knows you get a
meeting
To rest on your lap
When I sit on the floor
To look up to you
Without your full knowledge.
Admiration and devotion on
Plain view, you fain blindness.
Head in hands, I'll continue
In this torturous position.

POSITIONS (TAKE 2)

Do you know why I sit
On the floor?
To feel you're my master
It's you I adore.
I look up to you
This way.
Both physically and
Figuratively.
A pain swells, eyes drain.
Most desperately

UNTITLED 46

Abhor Abiding
Aberration Accepts
Complications Complying
Find rules quite inept.
Neglect Normality
Negotiate Never.
Initiate Violence
and sell yourself clever.

DRESSING UP IS NONSENSE

Flemping on a towel
on the rumpluff end of bed
staring into mirror
with a turban lonans on my head.
Powders, perfumes, slicks and
crambles out and on the side,
sprays and smell, colours
and colofers ready to collide
My skin is caked and biscuited
Too I'm not surgery and
gamble. I go to choose
shoes and dress for which
the choice is ample. Towel
gwelsing on the floor, as I slif
the fabric on my bones, 8 ¼
minutes to get ready, then
Brink Bring the taxi Phones.
Everybody else do.
Do it yourself
Work long... work work

THE PERFECT CHORE

As a lazy housemaid.
Ordered and told.
Dressed Impeccably
Sore for the under
Bane in appropriate places
laced in the other
shrouded in uniform
Regulation states such.
Vowed as an oath.
Contracted to give all.
Obliging and honest.
Details in entirety
But never believed.
As if the silverware
Went missing.
Obediently confused
Confusingly obedient.
A reaction leads to action
Repeated action leads to
an opposite reaction.
In consistency deadening
Punishment in emotion
Where emotion is punished
But none is seen as
a lack of will to obey

Scrupulously maintained
Not to the point of vanity
Just to please
Without opponent effort
The hours though are

plenty
Want of full capture untold
Life anxiously on hold
Arteries pump through a
Single vein.
Employer with all to gain.
Signed and dated
First site.
It may not be literal but
The hold is so tight.

Tender hooks
Tender blows
The game master knows
It's a game no one wins
Abundant and imagined sins.
The lazy housemaid

Commits no crime but if

This carries on she'll
Think she has in time.

I know what you did
What a terrible person you are
How you lie
And project you caricature onto me
Think and tell me I'm the waster.
As far as humans go

I'm innocent, my thoughts
Impure but voiced.
Trust fall.
It's a God-awful shame
that I love you.

(This was written
far before
I cheated on him-
I became what he
thought I was)

UNDERSTAND

The world doesn't
Spin without the
Propulsion of my hand.
And & roaches stare
at me.
Swearing they hate
But they're jealous
I'm free

UNTITLED 47

The heightened heat
he used to take
her protection to the floor.
And insert a memory
too disgusting to ignore
to prove to her
that she is too
degraded to adore.
But him and he and
men and you all but
do the same
You undress probe then
tuck away and black
mail with the shame
Ensuring herself wash
is much too low so
             she'll remain

RHETORIC TOWN

It's cascading mundane,
Fenestration opaque:
70's but without sign
of flare.

For with its elevation of the
member status
is too gain
Her head flushes red and
with a swarming rush
of desperate fear, she wanders
should she do what's
asked just to keep him
near?
Be brave and suffer
indignity and not
release a single tear
Did they know and does
He know she abhors the
way she looks and is seen
And photographs of
Wretched acts
remind her she's obscene
Wish faults displaced
the fat the scars,
worse than any other
the aim is to
the option
means that he won't
lover her.

CHERRY PICKED

Latticed lust pin pinched
with fear
Adams a brick blockage
that surrounds
her naivety and youth
til sick loves forcibly made
A wish for tools of mind
and body for which to get
that beast be stayed
replaced with submission as
hard as the sofa on
which she ungracefully laid.
Barely a garden of Eden,
those patchy brambles give heed and
perverted hormones spew from
retched bones.
The new
The bad, with stalls unboned.
The thief of truth
                    youth.
Knocks as before
Never does
But rears
Only a sticky
head to aim she
is a
WHORE.

UNTITLED 49

Taking sour sips
    from life's lush lips
Rocking hips
    in relationships
Keeping beat
with your blistered
        feet.
Ballet the words of the mocking birds
                            Singing

UNTITLED 50

Rain on my crape flower
Crafted by innocent
Hands

MY SISTER

I love my sister
She is perfectly miserable.
She screams when she thinks
I cannot hear,
She is a failure
A liar and a cheat
Because "she has to be"
But she has an air.
of solemn beauty
You only want to comfort her
She is grounding
She is humble
She is never arrogant
In fact she hates herself
She sucks the warmth
From every light.
She sees no hate
No future
I love my sister
Because she is helpless
In need of a master
Preferably a cruel one.
I love her because she
Is desperate to be loved.
But mostly I love her
Because she is part of me
Creativity
I have to kill my sister
....
But mostly I have to
Kill her because she

Is begging to die
My sister made me write
This.

I'M SO IN LOVE (VERSION 1)

You are a Cold Draft,
through a closed door.
You're a back of
Caution sign on a wet
floor.
You are the well deserved
cigarette flicked in the
eye,
The misplaced compliment
that made me cry.
You are all the names in
my bed,
The warm gap in my
Empty bed.
You are the paddle
that gets me wet.
You are the stranger
I never should have
met.
You are the gum
that shot the Dove.
It's lucky for you.
I'm so in Love

I'M SO IN LOVE (VERSION 2)

You are a cold draft
through the bottom of a
closed door,
you are the lack of caution
on a slippery floor.
You are the well deserved
 cigarette flicked in the
eye,
the misplaced compliment
that made me cry
you are all the names in
my head,
the warm gap, in my empty
bed
you are the puddle that
gets me wet.
You are the stranger I
Never
should have met. You are
the gun that shot the dove.
Its lucky for you I'm so in Love.

UNTITLED 52

He said this: yes, He did.
"I don't want to see you
upset"
"I care about you"

"Be with me properly.
See with me, undeniably
For right or wrong. For my
demons sit lighter when you're
 in my bed, and I'm facing
the other way. A little drop of
victory as a result of a girl,
a drop of wine and a single bed.
I'm fucked up and we all know
It, And I know it doesn't seem
This way but I have my work
…. A retractable but irreplaceable
World- irreplaceable tru

UNTITLED 53

Air ports are a bit of a mystery
The impersonality of a shopping
Centre, the boringness of a bus
Shelter and the occupants
Share the diversity of an internet
Chat room. The closest word
For descriptive purposes is purgatory
Not even in a comical
Kind of way but in a factual way
By which time freeze,
The climate is regulated to
A cool dry normal and every
race appears in every attire
to suit wherever they're going.

About this time of year
The norm is the British man
And women in such wanted
Anticipation of sun they brave
The chill air conditioning in
Sunglasses, shorts and sandals.
They've some expectation
They'll return from Spain, or
A Greek island as a buffed bronze deity like
Versions of their former selves.
In reality, and they forget
the truth each year they
return. Is that they'll
most likely gain a few
ice cream and alcohol

pounds, burn, and flake
and be covered
in itchy red swollen insect
bites. The image of which
I can only compare to an
Overfed, albino snake, shredding
It's skin, oh. With a rash.

We were not seeking the
Sun rays. Moscow was to be a cultural
Experience, fantastic photo
Opportunities and a get away
Without the tourism other
Cities bring.
I was not imaging the
Snow and ice of cliché
Russian setting, it's summer,
But I was expecting to
Need a jacket or at least an

Umbrella. We had checked
The weather online a few
Days before and still being
Informed of temperatures hitting
30C hadn't quite sunk in.
The Ibizan's of the previous page would have been jealous!

There isn't even a
Cool breeze apart from by

The river. Humidity soaring
Too. Having walked round
Rome in the height of
Summer and now the red
Square at may in summer
I'd happily and unashamedly
Compare the two.

Curiosity put the
Girl in lipstick and
Leather. Curiosity fucked the
Girl from her ass to
Head, gave her a grin
And called her "all grown up"
Then she feels like she knows
Enough about life to have an
Opinion... for a while. I know
Just how little I've experienced.
I know. But new I run.
I look for friends, when they're
Sat with cigarettes
The spiders down beside her
She pulled from her throat
A note.
It read;
I'm part of the nursery
My thoughts all in rhyme
I've crossed the lips of children
And mothers through time
Just a fable, need them
Put on the table
The fear of the most, an effortless
Ghost, who will not touch hearts
Only a story, I've written not
Real, people oblivious that
I may too feel.

She ran. Not physically, but she
Ran. She had started at some
Point about 18 months ago —
Striving for love, death and
All the sticky sick shit in-between
But now she'd simply terrified herself.

I wish I'd never opened
My eyes. I've heard it's
Fools that don't see the real
World- the fools are those that
Are happy but search for something
Else anyway. Curiosity didn't
Kill the cat, it cut the ribboned
Plaits off the little blonde girl.

1. Consumerism, money, relying on
   Possessions to make you happy
2. Alcoholism, drug addiction
3. Controlling relationships, giving your
   Soul to a love obsession
4. Depression, worthlessness, not living
   Because it doesn't feel worth it
5. Uncaring, social relationship disconnection
   To the point of robotism
6. Living only for survival, starving, homeless

Introduction: think of all the numbers of human
beings on
This earth, now think of all the people
you've ever met and ask yourself if
they were alive. Were they living life?
Ponder the intimate details of those 'lives'
You know best; are they happy, truly
And deeply content, in love with their
Existence and the world in which they exist?

UNTITLED 56

You are conflict
You know so
you've done the lot
the crack, the blow
and now you must
give up your life
line

drink, a thing you "should
mess" in time.
I am criminal
I am against the law
Despite the proof
And will
I've hit the wall
I'm addicted, I hate

Oh chaque feis
Les fuilles mortes
Tu repent a moun
Soureine
Jane apres joue
Les amours
Mortes
Ne'est finissent pas
Du moaine
Mais les chanxin est
Monotanne
A peu o peu mein
Indeffere – quelle que le
Le anuessentae
Ne' finsen pas matter.
y

BY JORGE

WHAT WAS LEFT

The hole that was left,
Was equal to a single,
Pound of flesh.

Extracted without blood,
Perhaps without pain,
All I know is that it was taken.

Higher is the price of a pound,
When it's all you have to give,
Yet the second is found.

Each day lived wholly,
Some hardly lived,
And some almost saw her end.

The exquisite mocking irony,
That saw her finish,
Off her terms.

Many days saw pain,
More still saw anger,
But all saw love.

You have company now,
So rest well,
In the knowledge,
You live still,
In this tome,

This declaration,
Of a genius.

By Jorge.

COST OF A MOBILE PHONE

One man
Hath two hands
One for the wheel
One for the phone.

One hand
Hath five fingers
Four curled around
Metal and plastic
One for the glass.

One man
Hath two eyes
Both for the road
Both for the phone.

The divided attention
Of superiority
The disregard
And arrogance absurd.

If you too could
Or rather could not see
The car
And hear the twisting
Snapping steel
Of a life less than half lived
Extinguished
Then the selfishness would
Stop
And it would not require lives lost

Or four and a half years of pain
For any party.

By Jorge

Printed in Great Britain
by Amazon